Series 536

WHAT TO LOOK FOR IN WINTER

by E. L. GRANT WATSON
with illustrations by C. F. TUNNICLIFFE, R.A.

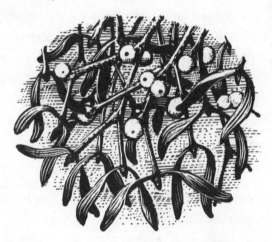

Publishers: Ladybird Books Ltd . Loughborough
© Ladybird Books Ltd (formerly Wills & Hepworth Ltd) 1959
Printed in England

WHAT TO LOOK FOR IN WINTER

The ivy, which flowers in December, gives a rich supply of honey to winter moths and those insects that survive the autumn. Drones, driven from their hives by worker bees, together with wasps and a large variety of flies, gather on the yellowish, pale-green blossoms. The nectar is intoxicating, and if one shakes the flower bunches, drunken insects fall buzzing to the ground.

In December many berries are ripe: holly, hips-and-haws, and the white snow-berries on their bare twigs. These have a soft, queer feeling when squeezed. If you look closely at the ivy, you will see amongst the flowers a few green berries forming; when they are ripe they have a beautiful, dark purple colour. In March they are greedily eaten by mistle-thrushes when most other berries have fallen or been eaten. Hedge-banks and ditches are russet with the browns and yellows of the dead bracken-fronds.

At this time the farmer begins to trim his hedges. He slashes the saplings half through, then bends and twists them between stakes into a firm fabric. Being alive, they continue to grow in springtime when the sap is again moving. No wind is blowing, and the distant trees show mistily in the winter air.

4

In woods and copses many leaves have fallen from the trees, although here and there an oak tree or a sapling beech will hold its leaves, though these are withered and dead. Near to the foot of the big beech trunk a log has fallen and is far-gone in decay. Two kinds of fungi and some green clumps of moss are growing on its slimy surface.

Under a protecting shelf a company of snails have taken shelter for the winter. They have sealed themselves into their shells with their own slime, and will not move until the spring sunshine tempts them out. Then the snails will unseal, and feel their way with sensitive horns extended, looking for food to break their long fast. On the nearby stump of the fallen tree some bracket-fungi are growing. These are hard and woody, and if broken off look rather like shells. They are nice things to take home.

The hard winter has not yet come, and many ferns are still green against the background of brown fallen leaves. Mosses gleam with a strange brightness. On the fence under the oak tree a cock pheasant and two of his wives are perching. They will have a dangerous time when sportsmen come shooting in the woods.

To the left of the stile a hawthorn tree, bent by the prevailing wind, has a rich harvest of berries. At its foot, amongst the bare branches of the hedge, some strings of bryony vine are already drooping and beginning to decay, but still hold their scarlet berries. On the near side, brambles have sprung up thick and luxuriant; their leaves are still green, though often they turn to glowing shades of purple, bronze and scarlet. Amongst and over the brambles, festoon thick sprays of traveller's joy, or old-man's-beard, as it is sometimes called. Their leaves have all fallen, but the seeds still cling. These have feathered awns which, when the seeds fall, float them on the wind to distant places, where they can make new plants.

Near to the ricks of corn, behind his house, the farmer has brought the threshing machine. He and his men are feeding it. One man has the very dusty job of raking away the shucks and chaff. Another is stacking the straw on a new rick which grows larger as the old rick grows smaller. In the stubble-field a flock of white geese is feeding on the grain that the gleaners have not been able to pick up.

On ponds and lakes waterbirds gather in flocks during the winter. In this particular lake there is a large flock of coots. They have smart, black plumage with white beaks which extend to their foreheads and look like bald, white patches. They are well adapted for swimming, with flanges on their toes that give good resistance to the water. Like their close relative the moorhen, they move from pond to pond, flying low and running across country. Sometimes coots find their way into big cities and towns, and on lakes and ponds in the parks they become quite tame and can be easily watched.

At the edge of the meer are bulrushes; the tall seed-spikes are tight and brown. The sedge grows quite as tall, and when the seed-heads grow thick and close, they make a lovely, tuneless song as the wind bends them.

In the alder branches above the reeds a flock of red-polls and siskins is feeding on what can be found in the crevices of the bark and in the dried seed-heads. These beautiful little birds usually nest and rear their young in Northern Europe. They come south in winter to avoid the cold and ice. They are not as common as they used to be, but when seen are often in large flocks.

The cows have got their rough winter coats to keep them warm, for they have to stand out in all weathers. The farmer's cowman is feeding them with kale that has been cut in another field and brought in a tilting cart, drawn by the tractor. The men wear their warm winter windcheaters, for the weather has grown colder.

With the cold north winds, fieldfares have come down from the semi-arctic regions where they breed, and a flock of them is flying overhead. When you see field-fares settled in the fields they look like large, grey-blue thrushes. By the ditch-side are the dried and brittle stems of cow-parsnip, with seed-heads like inverted umbrella frames; and red campion, with seed-heads like small, upside-down censers; also the yellow ragwort may, even so late in the year, bear an occasional blossom. Most flowers are withered by mid-December, and many leaves are turned yellow or brown. Some few, like those amongst the grasses, are half-decayed, only the veins remaining like delicate fairy skeletons.

The seeds of the cow-parsnip have a pungent, attrac-tive smell, and should you pick and bite one, you will find it tastes of earth, and autumn and sunshine, and several other things.

There has been heavy hoar-frost which whitens the roofs, the tree branches, and the grass haulms; it clings to the sides of foxglove stems, and defines the spiders' webs hanging between stems and fence.

The farmer has been spreading the cow-dung from his cattle-sheds. Chunks of it lie amongst the frosted grasses, and already many birds have come to peck for worms and insects. The black-and-white magpies with their long tails are easy to tell, and so are the wood-pigeons, two of which are on the ground, and two about to alight. The rooks, if they are more than one year old, have naked beaks, and have a fine, glossy-blue sheen on their black feathers. The jackdaws, and there are two or three amongst the flock that has come to peck over the manure, have grey hoods and black faces. There are some starlings too, and all these hungry birds have come to look for food on this cold morning.

The ash tree, though it has shed all its leaves, still holds its melancholy-looking groups of seeds, which the country people sometimes call ash-keys.

In the churchyard most of the trees and bushes are evergreens. The laurels are easily known by their shiny and glistening leaves, which on the undersides bear little cups of honeydew at the base of the larger veins. If these leaves are torn or crushed, they have a pungent and pleasant smell, something like almond icing.

Yew trees are often found in old churchyards. It is said that they were planted there in times when people used bows and arrows, so that their branches might be cut to make bows because they are very tough and strong. The leaves of the yew are poisonous, and cattle or ponies should not be allowed to eat them. The red and purple berries, that look like tiny jam-tarts, are also poisonous. Thrushes and blackbirds swallow a lot, but usually spew them up again. If you look near yew trees, you will see their spewings. The holm-oak, under which the old gardener is raking up leaves, is also an evergreen. Like the laurel it sheds its leaves, but not all at once, mostly in springtime. It is a fine growing tree, and easily distinguishable from the common oak to which it is related.

The Scots pine is a different kind of evergreen, and the leaves grow in pairs of thin, long needles. They have a lovely scent, and when they fall, the forest ants use them for building their nests. The evening sunlight is shining on the red bark.

Snow has fallen. During the day there has been a thaw, but now it is freezing again and icicles have formed where water has run down. In the holly tree, which is rich with red berries, fieldfares, redwings, and mistle-thrushes are busy feeding. The fieldfares are like thrushes, but larger and more blue in colour. The redwings are smaller than the common thrushes; they fluff out their feathers and so look larger than they are. Both fieldfares and redwings are winter visitors; they breed in the north and come south to avoid the cold weather.

In really cold winters the redwings die in large numbers, even in the southern counties. These birds often starve when the snow is too deep to allow them to scratch for the insects on which they largely feed, and are never known to come to any bird-table or eat any food proffered to them. They are shy, wild little birds, and halfway in size between a thrush and a robin.

On the tall, black poplar tree are several bunches of mistletoe. How mistletoe comes to grow on trees nobody knows for sure. Poplars and apple trees are the most likely hosts for this half-parasitic plant. If you can find out how mistletoe germinates, you will be a discoverer of one of Nature's secrets.

The lake is partly frozen. Where the water has been kept in motion by the swimming movements of the ducks, ice has not been able to form, and so they have made for themselves pools in which they can dive to look for things to eat. Standing on the ice are mallards, both drakes and ducks. In the near pool are widgeon, and in the distance, tufted duck. These birds move about in flocks in winter, from one pond or lake to another, and often the flocks mingle.

The herd of swans seen coming down towards the open water, with a wonderful whirring of their wings, are not the usual swans that we know so well, but are winter visitors from the North, probably from Russia. They are whooper swans and are slightly smaller than the common mute swans. Their bills are yellow and black, not orange and black, and they have no knob on the upper part of the bill, as have the mute swans.

Two herons are standing nearby. They look almost as though they are having a doze, but herons seldom doze; their large china-blue eyes are exceptionally watchful. A little snipe has just run out from among the tufts of frozen grasses. In the shallows where the ice meets the mud he may find some worms or water-snails to eat.

Bitter east winds have blown spray from the lake, and the water falling on nearby herbage and grasses has frozen into thick layers of ice, and this has built up gradually into curious patterns, glazed by the continuous frost.

The stoat in the foreground has his semi-winter coat; much of the brown on his back and the yellow on his belly has turned to white. As he jumps through the deep snow it is more difficult for him to be seen both by his enemies and by the lesser creatures, such as rabbits and mice on which he feeds. In arctic countries the stoat turns quite white, all but the tip of his tail, which remains black. He is then called an ermine, and his fur is valuable for edging the rich garments of dukes and duchesses. In spring and summer, however, he turns back into a stoat. He only turns white or half-white in very cold weather. No doubt he is hungry, and is on the look out for something to kill and eat.

The stoat has seen the great crested-grebe and the little grebes that are swimming on the lake, but knows he cannot get at them. Grebes are great divers and skilful swimmers. They can swim in the water with their heads just above the surface, and can rise and sink in the water at will. When grebes dive in search of fish, on which they live, they can stay under for a long time. If you wait and watch, you will be surprised to see how far away they come up again.

Snow has been falling for several days, and even in the woods it has covered all the ground. The rabbits can find no grass to eat, and so to still their hunger are gnawing the bark from young beech trees.

The deep footsteps in the snow show the marks made by their larger hind feet. A fox also has passed this way; from his tracks one can see that he was running: two footmarks, one in front of another, then a gap, then two more. A stoat has found the going difficult in the soft snow. You can see where his little feet have sunk, quite differently placed from fox or rabbit tracks.

A barn owl, who is no doubt hungry, since most of the mice are under the snow, is out hunting by daylight, hoping for some unwary small bird or a mouse who has ventured out to smell the upper air. The mice are safe under the snow and find their food in the moist, soft earth. Owls, since they eat so many mice, are one of the farmer's best friends. Mice are his enemies, since they eat his corn and gnaw his sacks, and eat the grubs of bees that fertilize the red clover. They do a great deal of harm. Owls, hawks and buzzards keep the mice in check.

Frost is still white on roofs and branches. A flock of small finches has settled in the branches of the thorn tree beside the Dutch barn. On both the lowest and topmost branch sits a greenfinch, and there are two other greenfinches in the group. Three bramblings, which are rather like cock chaffinches, but more brightly coloured, are on the upper twigs. These are winter visitors and breed further north.

Yellow-hammers might be mistaken for greenfinches, but they have a brighter yellow plumage. There are two sitting close together. The other finches in this flock are all cock chaffinches. During the winter months it is usual for chaffinches to go in flocks of cock birds or hen birds. The hen chaffinches are grey-green and do not have pink breasts. In the spring the flocks break up and then each bird finds its mate.

In the barn the farmer is slicing the hay with his sharp, broad-bladed knife. His man waits to load the hay into the cart. The horse waits patiently, his breath steaming in the cold air. His rough winter coat keeps him warm.

A red sunset on a frosty evening promises fine weather to come. Starlings are flying in converging flocks towards their roosting place in the trees beyond the lake. Already some are perching in the upper branches, but most of the flocks are slow to settle, and for a long while swoop to and fro, making curious patterns. Separate flocks are meeting to divide again, and all the while more birds will be alighting in the tree-tops. Their chatterings can be heard from far away, and so can the whirring of their passing wingbeats. As they settle they talk loudly in their starling language.

The evening flight of starlings is a most wonderful sight, and one that should always tempt us to linger and watch as the light fades and the air becomes colder. They take a long time to settle down for the night, since smaller flocks of late arrivals come to find places among the already heavily laden branches.

Magpies also gather together in winter and early spring at roosting-time; sometimes seven or eight to-gether; at other times as many as thirty or more. On the broken stump under the ash tree a wren, who goes to roost late, is looking to see what insects he can find amongst the cushions of moss and in the decaying wood.

The soil has thawed sufficiently to allow the farmer to start ploughing. He is sitting on his tractor that draws the four-furrow plough, and is glancing back at the gulls that follow to pick worms out of the upturned earth. They are black-headed gulls, which at this time of year have only a slight indication of the dark chocolate-brown hood that they will wear in springtime and summer. They call their harsh cries as they settle to pick out the good things that the blades have turned up.

A flock of lapwings is circling to come down and join in the feast. They have a flickering flight, made particularly noticeable by their broad, black and white wings. Some rooks have already settled on the furrows beside the gulls. You can tell them from crows or jack-daws by their white, naked beaks and their blue-black, glossy plumage. Young rooks in their first year have feathered beaks, and these are not so easy to tell from young crows.

Nearby a hare is running across the furrows and the strip of unploughed field. His greater size, and the dark tips to his long ears, easily distinguish him from a rabbit. Some snow is still lying on the distant hillside.

Two fields away a pack of hounds is casting for the scent of the fox who has just jumped over the log. He is aware of his danger, for he has been hunted before, so has doubled back in the opposite direction. The two men, who are cutting down the tree, have not seen the fox who has run quietly by, for they are looking at the hounds and huntsmen, and the following field.

Like all countrymen, they enjoy the sight of dappled hounds and the riders on their horses. In a moment or two the hounds are almost certain to get his scent, but this fox has a good chance of getting away, for he knows his country far better than the pack which follows him. Like most foxes he can be up to many a cunning dodge, and he will probably live to raid the farmer's hen-roost yet again.

The woodsmen are using axes on these beech trees, but later will use the cross-cut saw, as you can see from the stumps.

Two of the farm hands are uncovering a clamp of mangold roots to feed to the cows. A couple of mice, which were disturbed from their nest when the straw that covered the roots was pulled aside, are escaping into the grass. They are long-tailed field-mice, beautiful and easy to tame, but very destructive, and are consequently the enemies of farmers and gardeners. Like most mice they gnaw more than they eat, for if they do not gnaw, their teeth grow too long. They have to gnaw to live, and that is partly why they are so destructive. They also eat bumble-bee grubs, and bumble-bees are useful because they fertilize the red clover.

The roots are being loaded into a cart which will take them to the gate where the cattle are waiting, for they know where they will be fed. Sometimes the cows are fed on hay, sometimes on roots.

Over the meadow a kestrel hawk is hovering. With his large, bright eyes, that can see so far and so well, he is on the look-out for any mouse that may be so rash as to venture out. Kestrels and other hawks are farmer's friends, for they destroy many mice. It has been estimated that a single kestrel kills four thousand mice a year. Lucky for the two in the grass they are so far away.

In the enclosure, sheltered by the stone wall, some ewes have been lambing. The hay, which has been cut from the stack beyond the wall, has been pitched into a big wire trough. The sheep can pull at it through the wide meshes. They also have been gnawing turnips.

The sheep and their lambs look happy and contented, and rather like it when the jackdaws settle on their backs to pick the ticks from their skins. On the wall are five other jackdaws, two pairs and an odd one. Jackdaws are smaller than rooks, and not so glossy black; they have grey hoods and have hairs on their beaks; their cry is a 'clack' and not a 'caw'. In the thorn-tree two cock mistle-thrushes are fighting for the hen, who sits with her back turned as though she knew nothing about it, but is quite aware of what is happening.

On the far side of the stone wall is the stack from which the hay has been cut. Only about a quarter of it is left. Snow still lies on the distant hills, gleaming white in the light of late afternoon.

In the branches of larch that hang above the stone wall are three blue-tits and a great-tit. They move in short flights, and are searching the bare branches and the dried cones of last year for any small insects that may be hiding there. The blue-tits can creep like mice among the twigs, and can hang on in any position. The cat on the path is looking at them, as cats do at birds they cannot reach. The wall is coloured with lichens of various kinds and close-growing mosses. Polypod ferns grow in the crevices between the stones.

Last year's grasses are brown and withered, but an early periwinkle has a single blossom amongst its green leaves. The winter heliotrope is still in flower, and in this sheltered garden, the leaves which are often killed by the frosts of winter, still survive. A new crop will sprout with the coming springtime. These flowering heads, which are made up of groups of small flowerets, have a sweet, though somewhat sickly, scent.

They are in bloom from November till February, and although they have a beauty of their own, they are much disliked by gardeners. The plants spread by underground stems, called rhizomes, and in a short while will choke all other vegetation.

When we see the hazel catkins turn yellow, we know that spring is not far off. The catkins, sometimes called lambs' tails, are a drooping string of small flowerets that bear only stamens. Each flower produces a large number of pollen grains. These are wafted on the wind, and a few fall on the stigmas of the scarlet female flowers, which are too small to show in this picture. From the meeting of the male and female flowers, nuts grow slowly to ripen in September. At the base of the nut-sapling, honeysuckle vines are putting out their first, tender green leaves, another sign that spring is coming.

The blackbird has his springtime plumage, and very smart indeed he looks. His wife, who is away building her nest, is brownish, and does not have a yellow bill. The rooks in the elm-tops are beginning to show an interest in their last year's nests, which they will soon be rebuilding. The elm blossoms are beginning to show a purple tint, and will be even brighter coloured by early spring.

On the pasture a flock of green and golden plovers has settled. The green plovers have crested heads, and remain with us all through the year; but the golden plovers take long voyages to far distant lands. Two swans are swimming on the lake.

In the crevices of stone walls, in districts where stone walls form natural boundaries between fields or gardens, many plants take root. In any small area quite a number can be found. The wall pennywort, which has a round, fleshy leaf the size and shape of a penny, has early green leaves. Later in the year it puts forth a tall spike, bearing a large number of small flowers.

Hart's-tongue ferns grow in damp places, and are common on walls, and so are spleenwort ferns of several kinds. The two smaller ferns on this wall are black spleenwort.

In the soil at the base of the wall are the sprouting first leaves of the wild arum. These plants later produce curious complex flowers called 'lords-and-ladies', which have a device for catching flies. The tall spike, enclosed in the folded spathe, is slightly warm and attracts small flies to come and warm their feet. Later they are lured into the fold of the spathe from which they cannot escape until they are well dusted with pollen, and so are able to fertilize another plant.

Beside the wild arum is an early group of violets, which in this sheltered place have blossoms a week in advance of their usual time.

The farmer is sowing his corn in the large field that has been ploughed and harrowed. He drives his tractor while his man stands on the tilt, to see that the seeds run evenly. On the branches of a horse-chestnut tree three wood-pigeons are watching with personal interest. They are quite aware of what is happening, and are waiting for the time when it is safe to fly down to scratch up and eat the corn. Wood-pigeons eat a great many seeds of various kinds, and although they do some good for the farmer, they do much more harm. Consequently they are often shot at, and they know just as much about guns as they do about corn. They have grown wise in judging their chances.

The buds of the horse-chestnut are by late February swollen by the expanding leaves that they contain. A sweet-smelling, sticky substance protects the brown bracts. Early in March the characteristic five-fingered leaves will push aside the bracts and expand.

The finer twigs are those of a beech tree. Their narrow, lanceolate (or spear-shaped) buds are also covered by bracts, which in April will be cast off and wafted about by any breeze that blows. They litter the ground, and many will be blown in at cottage windows.

Heavy rains that often fall in February have flooded the low-lying meadows in the broad valley. Both the hedge and the wire fence are partly submerged, and the trees, which are growing on the far side of the fence that divides the flooded fields, are reflected in the still water. A flock of ducks, very easily distinguishable by their flight, is about to alight beside some of their companions already swimming in the flood-water. Gulls are circling or perching on the fence; they are on the look-out for the many drowning insects or worms that float on the flood-water.

In the foreground cluster springtime leaves of butter-cups. The big foxglove plant has also its new leaves growing from the centre. Around them the old leaves of last year still cling. Primrose plants have also put forth their small and unexpanded young leaves.

Beyond the bracken a tall gorse bush is in flower. Country people believe that all through the year flowers can be found on gorse bushes, and the saying is: "When the gorse is out of bloom, then is kissing out of fashion".

Snow has fallen again, as it will sometimes do in February. Snowy weather is not so cold as black frost, and it has not harmed the snowdrops and the early purple crocuses. The early purple iris is of the kind called *reticulata*, and blooms later than its close relation iris *stylosa*, which thrusts up its pale buds in December and January.

Yellow aconites are also in flower. Their erect stems are unbent by the snow, and their bright faces tell of the returning springtime. A sprig of jasmine has strayed down from the garden wall to overarch this rock garden.

If you watch the snowdrops as they come up in February, you will see that the buds point straight towards the sky when they are young, but before they open into flowers they bend their necks and look towards the earth. Many of the spring and summer flowers do this, and it is interesting to notice which ones.

The first bees that venture from their hives on mild days come to collect honey and pollen from snowdrops, crocuses and aconites.

Ivy berries have ripened and have turned from green to a blackish purple. There is some mystery about the germination of the ivy. Gardeners and botanists have found it difficult to grow plants from the seeds, even though planted with great care. Yet the ivy is constantly reproducing, and young plants spring up in many places. It is supposed that the seeds do not germinate unless they have first passed through the digestive tract of a bird, and maybe of some particular bird, such as the mistle-thrush. Perhaps that is so. We do not know.

After the snow has melted, western winds have brought mild weather, and when the sun shines many signs of springtime appear. A brimstone butterfly has ventured from hibernation, and looks as fresh in his covering of yellow scales as do the green ivy leaves on which he sits. So fresh do these early brimstone butter-flies look that they appear to have newly emerged. This is not so; they have been hiding in some safe place through the winter months, and are tempted out by the warm air.

The lesser celandine and yellow coltsfoot are in flower, and in the grasses partridges, which are already paired, will, before long, be nesting. A cock sparrow has a hen's .feather in his beak, and is busy helping Mrs. Sparrow to build her dreadfully untidy nest.

INDEX TO ILLUSTRATIONS AND TEXT